EXPLORING THE SOLAR SYSTEM

ASTEROIDS, COMETS & METEORS

GILES SPARROW

Heinemann
LIBRARY

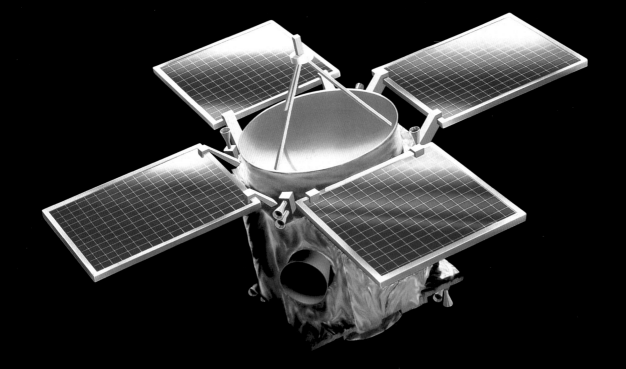

ASTEROIDS, COMETS & METEORS

Published by Heinemann Library,
a division of Reed Educational & Professional Publishing,
Halley Court, Jordan Hill,
Oxford OX2 8EJ, UK
Visit our website at www.heinemann.co.uk/library

Produced by Brown Partworks
Project Editor: Ben Morgan
Deputy Editor: Sally McFall
Managing Editor: Anne O'Daly
Designer: Michael LeBihan
Illustrators: Mark Walker and Darren R. Awuah
Picture Researcher: Helen Simm
Consultant: Peter Bond

© 2001 Brown Partworks Limited

Printed in Singapore

ISBN 0 431 12278 4 (hardback)   *ISBN 0 431 12279 2 (paperback)*
06 05 04 03 02 01   *06 05 04 03 02 01*
10 9 8 7 6 5 4 3 2 1   *10 9 8 7 6 5 4 3 2 1*

British Library Cataloguing in Publication Data

Sparrow, Giles
  Asteroids, comets and meteors. – (Exploring the solar system)
  1.Asteroids – Juvenile literature 2.Meteors – Juvenile literature 3.Comets – Juvenile literature
  I.Title
  523.5

BELOW: *The planets of the Solar System, shown in order from the Sun: Mercury, Venus, Earth, Mars, Jupiter, Saturn, Uranus, Neptune, Pluto.*

CONTENTS

*Some words are shown in bold, **like this**.*
You can find out what they mean by looking in the glossary.

Debris of the Solar System

The space between the planets of our Solar System is not empty. It is teeming with billions of tiny objects, ranging in size from specks of dust to balls of rock hundreds of kilometres across. This **debris** comes in three main types: asteroids, comets and **meteoroids**.

Eros is a typical asteroid. It has an irregular shape, and its surface is pitted with craters. The dark crater just below this caption is 5 kilometres (3 miles) wide.

Asteroids are lumps of rock not large enough to be called planets. The largest, Ceres, is 930 kilometres (578 miles) across, but most are much smaller. There are thousands that are a few kilometres wide, and billions the size of large boulders. All but the biggest are oddly shaped.

Most asteroids travel around the Sun in roughly circular **orbits** in the **asteroid belt** between the orbits of Mars and Jupiter. However, many orbit further out in the Solar System. Other asteroids travel in stretched, or **elliptical**, orbits that bring them closer to the Sun for part of the time. These are called Near Earth Asteroids (**NEAs**) because their elliptical orbits sometimes cross Earth's orbit.

Comets are chunks of dusty ice that orbit the Sun far away in the outer reaches of the Solar System. The only ones we usually get to see are the small minority that swoop through the inner Solar System from time to time. These travel around the Sun in highly elliptical orbits, taking them close to the Sun at one point and then far away again. As comets approach the Sun, sunlight heats them up and they develop an enormous cloud of gas and dust called a **coma**, as well as two or more glowing tails that grow millions of kilometres long.

Meteoroids are the smallest type of space debris. They range from dust left behind by comets to large chunks of broken-up asteroids. Meteoroids that enter Earth's **atmosphere** usually burn up in the sky. These are called **meteors** or shooting stars. Large meteoroids that pass through the atmosphere and hit the ground are called **meteorites**.

Imagine you're going on a **mission** to study space debris. Meteoroids are scattered throughout the inner Solar System, so they are easy to study from Earth. To study an asteroid or a comet you will have to go farther afield – in a spaceship.

Your flight will be designed so that it will take you close to several asteroids, and then alongside a comet. Your best bet is to fly to the asteroid belt, where about 10 billion chunks of rock orbit the Sun at an average distance of about 400 million kilometres (250 million miles). To intercept a comet you will turn back toward the Sun – because many comets pass near the Sun in their orbits, this should be a good place to find one.

Above: *The brilliant coma and long gas tail of Comet Hyakutake were clearly visible on its orbit close to the Sun in 1996.*

Below: *This diagram of the Solar System shows the planets orbiting the Sun. You can also see the asteroid belt (blue), the orbit of an NEA (red), and the highly elliptical orbit of a comet (green).*

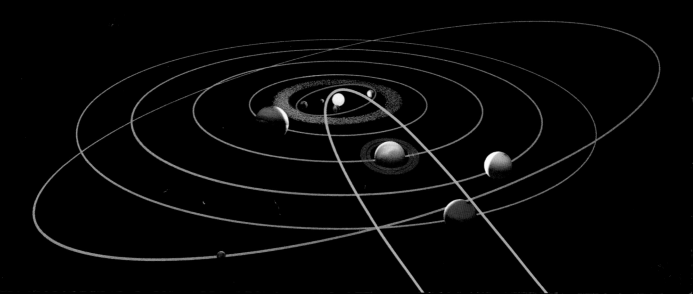

Through the asteroid belt

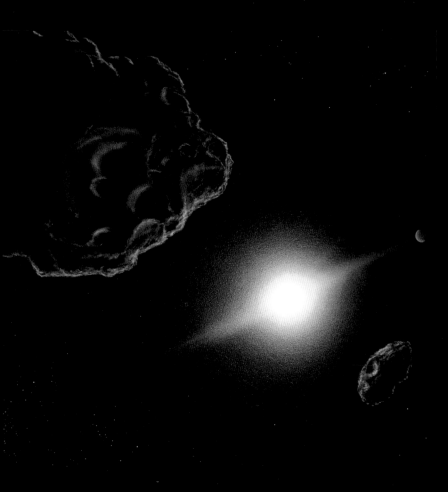

The journey from Earth has taken eight to nine months, and after a close **flyby** of Mars, you are finally approaching the inner edge of the **asteroid belt**. On your ship's charts the belt looks incredibly crowded, but the space through which the asteroids are travelling is so vast that you can rarely see more than one at a time. This is a good thing, because a head-on collision with an unexpected piece of space **debris** is definitely a recipe for disaster. However, it does make planning your trip more difficult, and you will have to plot a careful course through the belt to visit as many asteroids as possible.

This artist's impression shows two rocky, cratered asteroids orbiting within the asteroid belt between Mars (the red planet at the right) and Jupiter, with the Sun at the centre.

Even without landing, you can tell from their colours that there are several different types of asteroid. Some are brownish, some are red and others glint like metal. But the vast majority of asteroids are pitch black and visible only on your **radar** or silhouetted against the stars. As well as different colours, asteroids come in a huge variety of shapes and sizes.

Your first destination, Ceres, is the biggest asteroid of all and has a spherical shape. Only the largest asteroids have **gravity** that is strong enough to pull themselves into a ball – small asteroids tend to form irregular shapes. Several of the asteroids you fly past have moons in **orbit** around them, and in one place you even find a dumbbell-shaped asteroid made of two huge rocks orbiting each other and touching at a single point.

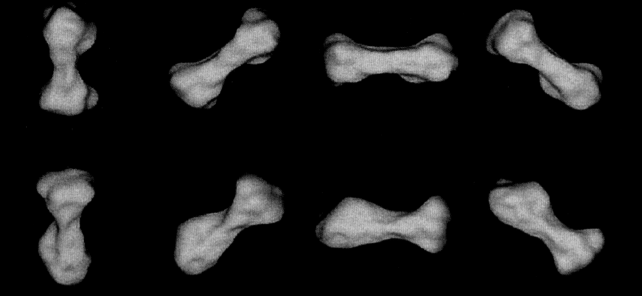

Asteroid 216 Kleopatra is about the size of Wales – too small to form itself into a sphere. These pictures from the Arecibo telescope in Puerto Rico show it at different angles as it tumbles through space.

In a couple of places you almost crash into a cloud of rubble – the remains of a large asteroid that was destroyed by a collision. When asteroids collide they split apart, and the fragments slowly spread out around the asteroid belt. Over thousands of years they create an asteroid family. Although the largest chunks are easy to dodge, the space between them is filled with countless tiny specks of dust travelling at extremely high speeds. These could cause damage if they hit your ship, so it's wise to avoid flying through the middle of an asteroid family.

The asteroid belt

Most asteroids are in the asteroid belt, which lies between the orbits of Mars and Jupiter. The belt contains circular gaps, named **Kirkwood gaps**, where it has been swept clear by Jupiter's gravity. There are also clusters of asteroids – the Trojans – within Jupiter's orbit. **NEAs** (such as the Apollos, Atens and Amors) orbit the Sun in paths that come close to Earth's orbit.

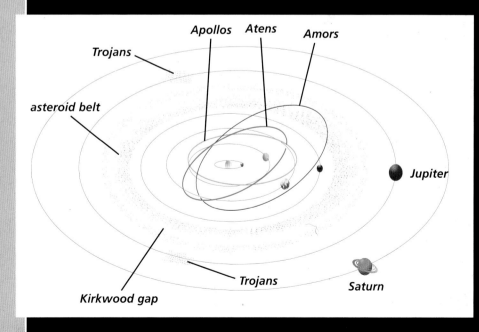

Ceres

Ceres is enormous for an asteroid. It contains a third of all the material in the **asteroid belt** and has stronger **gravity** than any other asteroid. As you go into **orbit** around Ceres, you see many craters on its surface. It looks like Earth's Moon, but it has none of the dark 'seas' found on the Moon. The edges of the **impact craters** are surrounded by lumps of rock called **ejecta**, thrown out by the collisions that formed the craters. Ceres is one of the few asteroids that has enough gravity to pull ejecta to its surface instead of letting it drift off into space.

ABOVE: Ceres was named after the Roman goddess of agriculture, shown here in a mosaic from the ruins of Pompeii, Italy.

BELOW: Although Ceres is the largest asteroid, it is tiny in comparison to Earth, as this artist's impression shows. Earth is about 13 times wider than Ceres.

Ceres

Earth

On the surface you feel very light. The gravity on Ceres is just a tiny fraction of even the Moon's gravity, and you can take leaps high into the sky, coming down more than a minute later. The sky is pitch black because Ceres has no **atmosphere**, and the horizon seems unnaturally close – you can see its curve clearly. You've come here to take a sample of the asteroid's dark, outer surface layer, which reflects only six per cent of the light falling on it. Your instrument pack tells you that Ceres's surface rocks are rich in chemicals containing carbon – the same **element** that forms graphite in pencils. The rocks also contain trapped water, bound up in the chemicals inside them. Although liquid water never existed on the surface of Ceres, you can tell that the material that formed this asteroid must have contained ice.

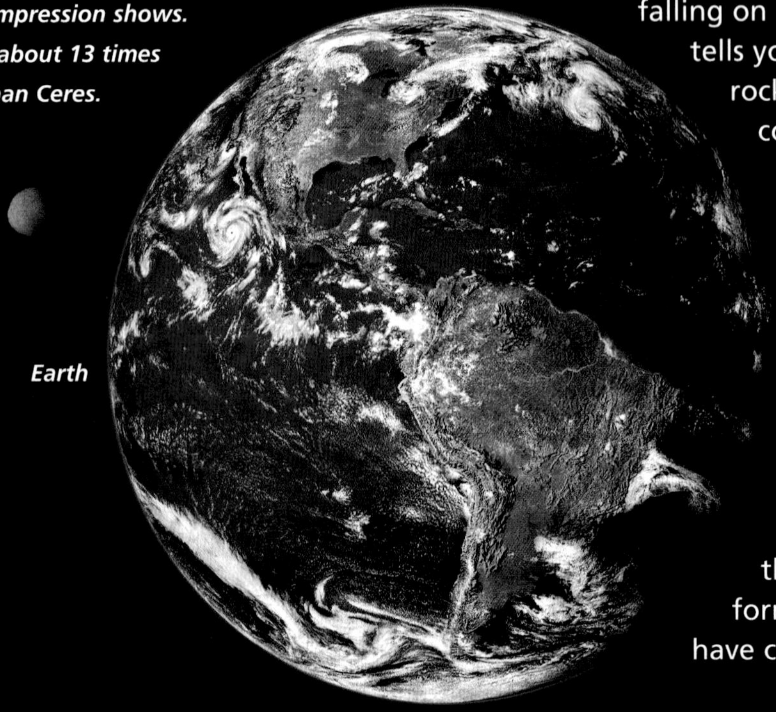

Mathilde

Your next target is Mathilde,
an average-sized asteroid about
55 kilometres (35 miles) across.
Roughly ball-shaped, some
of its edges have been
knocked off, forming
huge impact craters
up to 32 kilometres
(20 miles) wide.

Mathilde's surface is
just as dark as that of
Ceres, but you notice
one major difference.
Mathilde's weak gravity
means that the craters have
very sharp edges – all the
ejecta from impacts must
have been flung away into
space. In fact, the gravity seems
too weak for the asteroid's size.
Your ship's instruments show
that Mathilde must be very light.
A quick calculation shows it is only
slightly more **dense** than water.
The only explanation for this is that
Mathilde's interior must be full of spaces – perhaps
this asteroid is made from a jumble of rocks jammed
together with gaps between them.

This loose structure might actually have helped
Mathilde stand up to the impacts that scarred its
surface. Because **shockwaves** from a collision cannot
travel through empty space, they come to a stop in
the rocks around the gaps, instead of continuing and
tearing the asteroid apart. Many other large asteroids
might be rubble piles like Mathilde. Perhaps that is
why most big asteroids spin very slowly – if they spun
around faster they would pull themselves apart.

*Sooty carbon and other materials
in Mathilde make its surface pitch
black. This photograph from the
NEAR-Shoemaker **space probe**
has been enhanced to brighten
the surface features. Dark
asteroids like Mathilde are most
common in the outer regions of
the asteroid belt.*

Eros

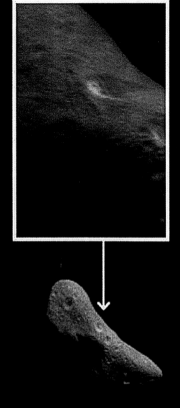

Your final stop in the asteroid belt is Eros, an **NEA** (Near Earth Asteroid) that is now at the outermost part of its **elliptical orbit**. At 34 kilometres (21 miles) long by 13 kilometres (8 miles) wide, Eros is smaller than Mathilde and irregularly shaped. It bulges at both ends, and its middle is pinched together in a saddle shape.

Eros's surface is paler than that of Mathilde and Ceres but just as heavily cratered. Landing near a large, pawprint-shaped **impact crater**, you step outside in your spacesuit to take some rock samples. **Gravity** is very weak here, and you need weighted boots and a weight belt to keep you from drifting away into space. The ground is crunchy underfoot – Eros is covered by **regolith**, a layer of dust and small rocks thrown out by **meteorite** impacts. The asteroid's strange shape does odd things to the weak gravity. The pull of gravity is slightly stronger on the bulges than in the saddle, and small rocks dislodged by your feet appear to roll uphill as you walk.

Your instruments reveal why Eros is a different colour from other asteroids you've seen. Its surface is rich in **minerals** such as silica – the mineral found in sand on Earth. After splitting a rock open with a pickaxe, you discover that the minerals inside the rock have formed into delicate spheres, called **chondrules**.

ABOVE: *A closeup of Eros reveals a huge, pawprint-shaped crater.*

BELOW: *Deep craters and boulders up to 30 metres (100 feet) wide – the bright, round objects on the right – cover the surface of Eros.*

How the asteroids formed

Discovering asteroids

Because very few asteroids are visible to the naked eye, it's not surprising that the first ones were discovered only after the invention of the telescope. Even then, the discovery of the first asteroid, Ceres, was accidental.

The asteroid Eros was named after the Greek god of love.

Ceres was first seen by the Sicilian astronomer Giuseppe Piazzi (1746–1826) on New Year's Day of 1801. Piazzi was constructing the most accurate sky map of the time, and as part of his careful method he would always measure the position of a star on two separate nights. This was how he discovered that one faint 'star' had moved, and must actually be within the Solar System.

At the time, many astronomers were already looking for a missing planet somewhere in the gap between Mars and Jupiter. Piazzi wanted to be sure before he announced his discovery, but he fell ill at a crucial moment and lost his planet in the Sun's glare. It was eventually rediscovered with the help of a group of astronomers named the celestial police, who had formed just a few months earlier to find the missing planet. They called in a brilliant young German mathematician called Karl Friedrich Gauss (1777–1855), who worked out a new way to calculate **orbits** from just a few observations. The new 'planet' was rediscovered on 31 December 1801, and Piazzi named it Ceres after the Roman goddess of agriculture.

However, many astronomers thought that Ceres was too faint to be a large planet, and the celestial police continued their search. In 1802 the asteroid Pallas was discovered, followed by Juno in 1804 and Vesta in 1807.

The German mathematician and astronomer Karl Gauss is shown in this engraving, completed the same year he died. His mathematical calculations of orbits led to the first discovery of an asteroid – Ceres.

Over the next few decades, hundreds more of these objects were discovered, and British astronomer William Herschel (1738–1822) named them asteroids, which means 'starlike objects'.

Most professional astronomers found asteroids a nuisance – they were hard to tell apart from stars, and they often formed streaks on photographs that blocked the view of more distant space objects. For these reasons asteroids were called the 'vermin of the skies' and, until quite recently, only amateur astronomers took any interest in discovering and cataloguing them. All this changed when professionals began to realize that **NEAs** might be a threat to Earth, and **flybys** by **space probes** began to reveal how much these small objects could tell us about the origins of the Solar System.

Asteroid names

Asteroids are the only space objects that the discoverer has the chance to name. The first ones were named after ancient Greek and Roman gods and goddesses, but more than 10,000 asteroids are known today, and such names ran out long ago. Today asteroids are often named after the families of their discoverers, famous scientists (such as Carl Sagan), or even rock stars (such as John, Paul, George and Ringo – the members of the Beatles).

Fictional characters are also allowed. Asteroid number 9007 is called James Bond after the famous British spy (above) invented by novelist Ian Fleming.

Missions to asteroids

The first **space probe** to fly past an asteroid was NASA's *Galileo* probe during its **mission** to Jupiter. *Galileo* encountered Gaspra in 1991, then Ida and its tiny moon Dactyl in 1993. The images taken by the probe were intriguing, but *Galileo*'s **flybys** were very brief, and the probe returned limited information about the asteroids.

In 1996 NASA launched *NEAR-Shoemaker*, the *Near Earth Asteroid Rendezvous* probe. It was the first probe designed specifically to study asteroids. Weighing 803 kilograms (1770 pounds), it was powered by solar panels and fitted with six instruments, including a camera, two **spectrometers** for identifying surface chemicals, and a **magnetometer** for detecting **magnetic fields** around asteroids. *NEAR-Shoemaker* made flybys of Eros and Mathilde before returning to Eros on Valentine's Day 2000 and going into **orbit** around the tiny world. In May 2000 the probe's instruments recorded Eros being hit by a high-energy **solar flare** from the Sun, causing the asteroid's surface to give out **X-rays**. These confirmed that Eros is a mixture of heavy and light materials and probably dates back to the origin of the Solar System.

There are plenty of plans for more probes to visit asteroids. One of the most ambitious is *MUSES-C*, a Japanese probe that will collect a sample of material from the surface of asteroid 1998 SF36 and bring it back to Earth. *MUSES-C* will also release a NASA-built robot that has a device to flip it around the asteroid's surface in the low **gravity**.

This compilation of two photographs, taken by the Galileo *spacecraft, shows the asteroids Gaspra (left) and Ida (right) to scale.*

The *Near Earth Asteroid Prospector (NEAP)*, a privately funded probe planned for launch in 2002, is aimed at the 1.6-kilometre-wide (one-mile-wide) asteroid Nereus. Astronomers think it might be possible in the future to mine asteroids like Nereus for their resources. The asteroid belt is a potentially huge source of metals and other materials. If even one asteroid could be dismantled and sent back to Earth in bits, it could revolutionize the world economy. According to some scientists, a typical small asteroid like Nereus could provide billions of dollars worth of iron, nickel, cobalt and precious metals such as platinum. Even the most common metals in asteroids could be valuable for space construction projects, because they would not have to be launched into space from the surface of Earth.

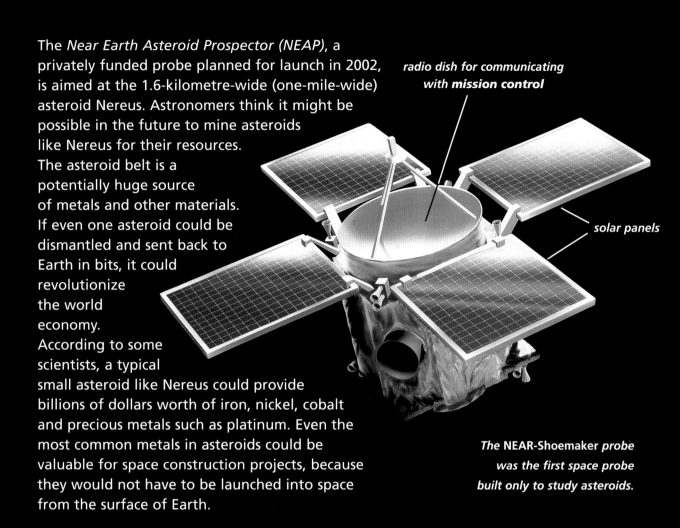

radio dish for communicating with mission control

solar panels

The NEAR-Shoemaker probe was the first space probe built only to study asteroids.

Eugene Shoemaker (1928–1997)

The NEAR-Shoemaker probe is named after Eugene Shoemaker, an astronomer and geologist from the United States who pioneered the use of geology to understand other worlds. Shoemaker's health prevented him from becoming an astronaut, but he helped analyse results from many of NASA's space missions and also discovered several comets.

Ride on a Comet

It's time to leave the **asteroid belt** and head back to Earth. According to **mission control**, a large comet is heading towards the inner Solar System and will pass close to you in a few days. Perhaps you can hitch a ride.

When the comet comes into view, you're disappointed. You were expecting to see a glowing white ball with a magnificent tail, but all you see is a massive black boulder tumbling slowly through space, without a tail. In fact, it looks just like an asteroid. Comets travel along stretched, or **elliptical**, **orbits**. This one's orbit is so elliptical that it appears to be heading directly towards the Sun.

You steer your ship into orbit around the comet. It's about 10 kilometres (six miles) wide, and the dark surface is pitted with **impact craters**. How is this going to turn into a ball of light with a blazing tail? Perhaps the surface will offer some clues. You land on the comet's dark side, but even your ship's powerful floodlights can hardly illuminate the black landscape.

Your first view of the comet might look something like this artist's impression of Comet Hale-Bopp – a dirty snowball with craters. This is how a comet looks during most of its orbit around the Sun. It is only when it gets close to the Sun that the ice vaporizes and forms a bright head and tail.

There's just enough **gravity** to walk across the surface. Your boots crunch on the loose ground, kicking up clouds of sooty dust, and within minutes the dust has turned your white spacesuit grey. You bend down to dig up a sample of dust, but the gravity is so low that you trip up and start spinning round. After anchoring yourself to the ground with a rope and metal peg, you collect a jarful of comet dust. Beneath the sooty surface the ground is made of paler material – ice with dust mixed into it.

You decide to visit the sunlit side of the comet. You leap over the surface in long, slow bounds that take you into the light. The Sun is dazzling here, but the sky is still black – except in one place, where there's a faint glow on the horizon. Another leap brings its source into view. A fountain of gas and ice is bursting out of the ground and glowing in the light. The comet has begun to wake up.

This spectacular photograph of Comet Hyakutake shows the brilliant head and tail a comet develops when it gets close to the Sun. Comet Hyakutake was one of the brightest comets of the 20th century.

Fred Whipple (born 1906)

The first person to suggest comets might be 'dirty snowballs' was astronomer Fred Whipple from the United States. Whipple discovered six new comets while working at Harvard College Observatory. Astronomers already knew there was gas in the tail of comets, and Whipple suggested that this gas was released as the icy heart of the comet began to melt.

Towards the Sun

As the weeks pass and the comet gets closer to the Sun, it gets more active. The sooty black lump you landed on – the comet's **nucleus** – is gradually warming up, and the subsurface ice is thawing. But liquids cannot exist in the **vacuum** of space, so the ice changes directly into gas and bursts out of the nucleus in jets. Back in orbit around the comet, you watch as new jets begin to erupt.

You've been hard at work analysing the samples you took from the nucleus, and the results are interesting. The sooty dust is made of a surprising range of substances, including rock dust, sulphur chemicals and **organic compounds**. The ice, however, is mostly frozen water, but it also contains frozen carbon monoxide and frozen carbon dioxide, or **dry ice**.

The sky outside the ship has become misty as more gas spews out of the nucleus. This growing ball of gas and ice grains is called the **coma**. Comet comas can grow up to 160,000 kilometres (100,000 miles) wide – eight times wider than Earth. If you could see this comet from Earth, the coma would now be visible as a glowing white dot in the night sky.

The coma of Comet Hyakutake formed a gigantic white ball, with the nucleus hidden deep inside its heart.

You've learned as much as you can from the comet's nucleus, so you decide to fly further out for a better view and travel alongside the comet.

*Comet Hyakutake appears over a forest in Alaska in 1996. The green light high in the sky is the **aurora**, or northern lights.*

Comet Hale-Bopp passed Earth in 1997 and was clearly visible to the naked eye, even over murky city skies. Here you can see its two main tails: the gas tail (blue) and the dust tail (white).

As you cross the **orbit** of Mars, the comet's glowing tail begins to develop. Your instruments reveal that the tail is made from gas and dust from the coma that have been blown across space by the force of the Sun's energy. From a distance you can actually see two tails: a narrow blue tail and a larger, yellowish-white tail. The blue tail is made of gas blown from the coma by the **solar wind** – an invisible stream of **particles** blasted out of the Sun. It glows blue because the solar wind makes the gas atoms emit light. The yellow tail is made of dust blown by the Sun's **radiation**, and it glows from reflected sunlight.

A comet's tail

*Comets look as though they are flying so fast that their tails stretch behind them, but that's just an illusion. The tails always point away from the Sun because of the force of the Sun's radiation and solar wind. The gas tail points in a straight line directly opposite the Sun, but the dust tail curves around a little because it is attracted by the Sun's **gravity**. Comets containing a lot of dust sometimes develop a faint third tail made of sodium **atoms**, but this is only visible through powerful telescopes. Comet Hale-Bopp, the biggest and brightest comet since 1811, was the first comet seen to have a sodium tail.*

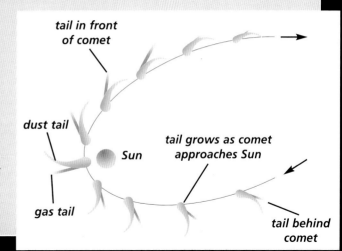

tail in front of comet

dust tail

Sun

gas tail

tail grows as comet approaches Sun

tail behind comet

Comet reservoirs

The comet you landed on is travelling in a very long, narrow **ellipse**. It will swoop close to the Sun and then fly back out into the outer reaches of the Solar System. According to your calculations, it won't be back again for another 500,000 years! What would you find if you could stay with it on its long, slow journey into outer space?

Far beyond the planets lies a huge reservoir of comets called the Oort cloud. This cloud may contain as many as six trillion comets in a vast sphere around the Solar System, and its outer edge is estimated to be 100,000 times further from the Sun than Earth is. At this phenomenal distance the Sun's **gravity** is so weak that comets are easily disturbed by passing stars or by the changing gravity of the **galaxy** itself. When a comet is disturbed, it may drift away into deep space or head towards the Sun.

ABOVE: *This artist's impression shows the Oort cloud – the cloud of comets surrounding the Solar System. The Sun and planets are located in the centre but are too small to show on this scale.*

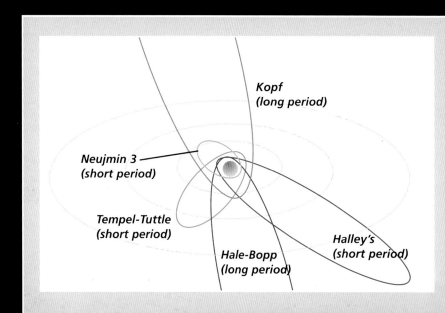

Kopf
(long period)

Neujmin 3
(short period)

Tempel-Tuttle
(short period)

Hale-Bopp
(long period)

Halley's
(short period)

Comet orbits

Comets have highly elliptical orbits that take them above and below the plane of the Solar System. Long-period comets, such as Hale-Bopp, come from far out in the Oort cloud on orbits that last for thousands or millions of years. Short-period comets, such as Halley's Comet, visit the inner Solar System much more frequently because their orbits are shorter.

How did the comet reservoirs form?

Astronomers think comets formed around 4.5 billion years ago, shortly after the Solar System was born. The Solar System formed from a vast cloud of dust and gas that shrank due to gravity. Most of the material ended up in the Sun, but the leftovers became planets, asteroids and comets. The comets developed from ice that collected in the freezing outer Solar System. When the planets formed, their gravity catapulted most of the comets out into space, forming the Oort cloud, as shown in this artist's impression. The comets that were left behind formed the EKB.

Comets from the Oort cloud that head towards the Sun end up on long, **elliptical** orbits around the Solar System. They are known as **long-period comets** – the comet you visited is a typical example. Like all long-period comets, its visits to the inner Solar System are very rare.

Other comets, known as **short-period comets**, make a regular appearance in the inner Solar System. These don't come from the Oort cloud but from a region of space called the **Edgeworth-Kuiper belt** (EKB). Unlike the Oort

Understanding comets

Although comets have been seen throughout human history, until 500 years ago astronomers thought they were part of the weather and well within the **orbit** of the Moon. It was not until 1577 that Danish astronomer Tycho Brahe (1546–1601) showed that comets were much further away, travelling on **elliptical** paths around the Sun.

Comets were studied with great interest, yet they were still a mystery. Astronomers figured out that a comet's tail always points away from the Sun and grows longer as it gets closer, but no one knew where comets came from or where they disappeared to.

In 1705 the English astronomer Edmond Halley (1656–1742) compiled a list of comets and their orbits, based on observations stretching back to the 1300s. Halley noticed that three comets seen in 1531, 1607 and 1682 had identical orbits, and suggested they might be one comet with a 75.8-year orbit. He was proved right when the comet (named Halley's Comet in his honour) returned, as predicted, in 1758. Other returning comets were soon identified, and orbits for some of them were calculated.

Tycho Brahe was one of the great astronomers of the pre-telescope era. He catalogued 777 stars, and his calculations helped his assistant, German astronomer Johannes Kepler, to prove that Earth orbits the Sun.

Some comets continued to turn up unexpectedly, however. Donati's Comet of 1858, for example, was probably the most studied comet of the nineteenth century – at its peak it outshone all but the brightest stars. More importantly, it was discovered while it was still a good distance from the Sun, which gave astronomers the opportunity to watch what happened during its approach.

ABOVE: *This computer-enhanced image of Comet Kohoutek was taken from the* Skylab *space station in 1973.*

As astronomers drew and mapped its constantly changing appearance, they discovered jets of gas emerging from its **nucleus** and ripples spreading rapidly along its tail.

Astronomical techniques improved throughout the nineteenth and the twentieth centuries, and it became possible to identify the chemicals that make up comets. This could be done by analysing the light coming from them – a technique known as **spectroscopy**. Surprisingly, comets turned out to contain large quantities of **volatile** chemicals, which evaporate as comets approach the Sun. This discovery led to Fred Whipple's 'dirty snowball' theory, which was proved correct when **space probes** finally visited comet nuclei.

Short- and long-period comets

The length of comet orbits varies enormously. Halley's Comet (below right) is a typical **short-period comet**. *Its orbit carries it out just beyond Neptune, and it returns to the Sun every 76 years. There are 135 known short-period comets, the shortest of which orbits the Sun in just three years. Because they return to the Sun so often, short-period comets tend to lose their gas and ice rapidly and become fainter with time. One* **NEA**, *called Phaethon, is in fact a* **dead comet**. *Long-period comets can have orbits lasting thousands of years, and are often much larger and more brilliant.*

Famous comets

In 1304 the Italian artist Giotto

Throughout history, people have seen comets as omens of disaster or great events. No one knows exactly how this association was first made – perhaps a comet just happened to be in the sky when a natural disaster struck. Whatever the cause, comets have always been viewed with superstition, and their appearances have often been recorded.

The most famous of all is Halley's Comet. It is by far the brightest **short-period comet** and was recorded many times before Edmond Halley 'discovered' it. Probably its best-known record is in the Bayeux Tapestry, where it is shown as a sign of the coming Norman Conquest of England in 1066. The Italian artist Giotto di Bondone was inspired by the comet's appearance in 1301 to show it as the Star of Bethlehem in

Every year several **long-period comets**
arrive unexpectedly from the outer
reaches of the Solar System. Most are not
visible to the naked eye, but some are truly
brilliant, outshining Halley's Comet and
even becoming visible in daylight. The last
daylight comet was seen in 1910, the same
year Halley's Comet returned. Bright, nighttime
comets appear more often – about once every
twenty years on average. One of the most recent
was Hale-Bopp, which passed by the Sun in 1997 and
was a spectacular sight. Its **coma** was brighter than
most stars, and its long tail stretched across the night sky.

In 1994 Comet Shoemaker-Levy 9, already ripped to
shreds by Jupiter's **gravity**, collided with the giant planet.
Although the impact happened on Jupiter's far side and
was not visible from Earth, clouds of gas from the
explosions rose high above the planet's edge, and Jupiter's
face looked 'bruised' for days afterward. The crash
showed for the first time that comets might be fragile.
Comets that get very close to the Sun sometimes break
up, and now we know that Jupiter's gravity can have the
same effect. Some comets disintegrate for no obvious
reason – this happened to Comet Linear in 2000.

*The impact site (the
dark area on the left) of a
fragment of Comet Shoemaker-
Levy 9 can be seen in this Hubble
Telescope picture of Jupiter after
the collision on 18 July 1994.*

Missions to comets

The **nuclei** of comets are difficult to study from Earth because they are hidden deep inside their glowing **comas**. The only way to get a good look at a comet, therefore, is to send a **space probe** into the coma. The first **mission** to a comet took place in 1985, when NASA sent a probe called the *International Cometary Explorer* through the gas tail of Comet Giacobini-Zinner. Data sent back to Earth from the probe revealed that the comet's nucleus was only about 2.5 kilometres (1.6 miles) wide.

In 1986 a fleet of probes visited Halley's Comet during one of its regular visits to the inner Solar System. Two Soviet, two Japanese and one European probe arrived at the comet during the same week in March. The Soviet *Vega 1* and *2* probes flew within a few thousand kilometres of the nucleus and photographed the coma. The Japanese *Suisei* and *Sakigake* missions passed further from the comet, studying how it affected the space around it.

ABOVE: *The Giotto probe took this picture of the nucleus of Halley's comet. It shows the bright jets of gas and dust that form the coma.*

BELOW: *This artist's impression shows Giotto on its way to meet with Halley's Comet.*

The last of the fleet to visit Halley was the European probe *Giotto*, which plunged straight into the coma and passed within 596 kilometres (370 miles) of the nucleus. *Giotto* got close enough to take pictures of the nucleus through the misty cloud of gas and dust surrounding it. The probe revealed a dark, irregular lump of rock and ice about 16 kilometres (10 miles) long and 8 kilometres (5 miles) wide. *Giotto*'s scientific instruments returned valuable information to Earth, but just 14 seconds before the closest approach, disaster struck. The probe was hit by a tiny grain of dust that destroyed the camera and cut off contact with **mission control**. Fortunately, the scientists managed to regain control, and *Giotto* went on to fly past another comet in 1992.

ABOVE: *This was one of the first pictures of the nucleus of Halley's Comet to be returned by* Giotto. *The dark region on the right corresponds to the shaded area of the nucleus on the opposite page.*

Several new comet probes are currently being built or are already on their way to various **short-period comets**. NASA's *Stardust*, launched in 1999, will return to Earth **orbit** in 2006 carrying dust grains from the tail of Comet Wild 2, while *Contour (Comet Nucleus Tour)* will study two or even three comet nuclei. The European *Rosetta* probe will launch in 2003 and travel for eight years to meet up with Comet Wirtanen in the outer Solar System. It will drop a **lander** on the comet's surface and then travel alongside the comet to record what happens as it wakes up and becomes active. Another proposed mission is 'Deep Impact', a plan to fire a 500-kilogram (1100-pound) copper missile into comet Tempel 1 to create an **impact crater** and find out what the comet's interior is like.

BELOW: *The* Stardust *probe, shown in this artist's impression, is on the way to Comet Wild 2.*

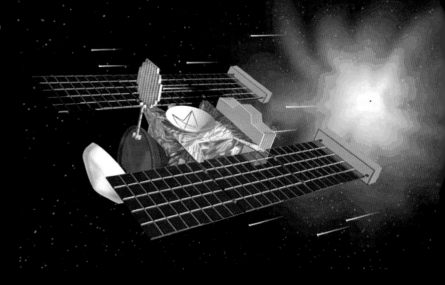

Shooting stars and meteor showers

You've now left the comet behind and have returned to Earth, but even from here you can see signs of the many small objects that clutter our Solar System. On a dark night, as you stare up into the starlit sky, a flicker of movement catches your eye – a star seems to have detached itself from the rest and zipped across the sky before disappearing. You wait a few minutes and see another, this time brighter and with a glowing yellow tail. These are shooting stars, or **meteors**.

Meteors are tiny, ranging from the size of a sand grain to that of a pebble. Yet they slam into Earth's **atmosphere** at such terrific speed – up to 266,000 kilometres an hour (165,000 miles an hour) – that they burn up in fireballs that are visible from kilometres away. The larger a meteor is, the longer it lasts and the bigger the fireball. All meteors are over in a flash – usually less than a second.

A shooting star, or meteor, was captured accidentally in this photograph of the aurora. Earth puts on about 550 tons in weight each year thanks to meteors.

Major meteor showers

Meteor showers happen when Earth crosses the path of a comet. Most happen at the same time every year and can be linked to particular comets. They are usually named after the **constellation** from which they appear to come, such as the Perseids (left), which come from the constellation Perseus.

NAME	DATES	PARENT COMET
Quadrantids	1–6 January	Unknown
Eta Aquarids	1–10 May	Halley's Comet
Delta Aquarids	15 July–15 Aug	Unknown
Perseids	23 July–20 Aug	Comet Swift-Tuttle
Orionids	16–27 October	Halley's Comet
Leonids	15–20 November	Comet Tempel-Tuttle
Geminids	7–15 December	Asteroid 3200 Phaethon

On most nights there are about ten shooting stars an hour, but tonight is different. Earth is moving through the trail of dust left by your comet, and shooting stars are appearing about once a minute. Astronomers call this a meteor shower. The number of shooting stars in a meteor shower reaches a peak at about 4 A.M., when the part of Earth you're watching from is moving directly into the dust trail as Earth rotates. Before midnight you're on Earth's **trailing side**, and only the fastest meteors become shooting stars.

Most of the shootings stars seem to be spreading out from one point in the sky, called the radiant. This is an illusion. The radiant occurs because all the meteors are travelling in the same direction through space. For the same reason, a long, straight road appears to narrow to a point in the distance.

Meteor storms

When a comet passes the Sun it leaves a fresh dust trail behind it that can cause heavier meteor showers for a few years afterward. If Earth passes through the dense centre of the fresh dust stream, there can be a spectacular meteor storm, with thousands of shooting stars every hour. The Leonid meteors produce a meteor storm every 33 years, and the last one was in 1999.

Meteorites

A meteorite strikes the ground in this artist's impression. About 500 meteorites hit Earth each year on average. Most fall in deserts, oceans or other uninhabited areas and are never found.

Occasionally a large chunk of interplanetary rock survives the burning heat of entry into Earth's **atmosphere** and makes it all the way to the ground. Lumps of space rock found on Earth are called **meteorites**.

As far as astronomers know, comets do not contain large chunks of rock, so where could meteorites come from? Asteroids are a likely source, because many meteorites are made up of materials that are similar to those found in asteroids. Some meteorites may be pieces broken off **NEAs** by collisions, but astronomers think most have been swept out of the **Kirkwood gaps** in the **asteroid belt** by Jupiter's **gravity**. A few meteorites seem to be chunks blasted off other worlds, including the Moon and Mars.

Most meteorites fall into one of four classes: chondrites, achondrites, irons and stony-irons. Chondrites are lumps of rock containing spherical objects called **chondrules**. Scientists think chondrules formed as tiny **molten** droplets in the cloud of gas and dust that circled the Sun when the Solar System was forming. In other words, chondrules are time capsules from five billion years ago. Some chondrites seem to have been changed by heat or moisture, and others are rich in **organic compounds**. There is a huge variety of chondrite meteorites, each type made up of different combinations of chemicals. The various types can often be matched to specific types of asteroid. The asteroids Ceres and Eros, which you visited earlier, are made of different types of chondrite.

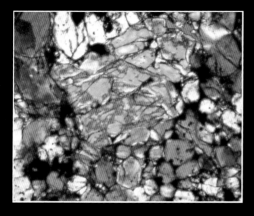

A chondrite meteorite, viewed through a microscope, shows chondrules inside it.

Achondrites are rarer than chondrites. In these meteorites the chondrules have melted together to form a single lump of rock. Achondrites could only have formed in the hot interiors of large asteroids, and some have been traced back to their origin in the asteroid Vesta.

Iron meteorites are lumps of metal, usually iron and nickel. They probably formed originally in the molten **cores** of **planetesimals**, and they often contain huge crystals of metal that froze as the cores cooled and solidified. Stony-irons are the rarest meteorites. They consist of rock crystals embedded in metal, and they may have formed around the edge of planetesimal cores.

This fragment from an iron meteorite fell in Siberia, Russia, on 12 February 1947.

A stony-iron meteorite shows a mixture of rock crystals (yellow) and metal (grey).

Meteorite hunting

Geologists travel to the most hostile parts of the world in search of meteorites. In most places it's very difficult to tell meteorites from normal rocks unless you see them fall, but in some places they stand out.

*In the 1960s Japanese scientists found meteorites lying on the snow in Antarctica. Since then, thousands more Antarctic meteorites have been found, including the Martian meteorite ALH84001 (right) in 1984. In 1996 scientists found tube-like structures inside ALH84001 that they thought might be **fossils** of tiny organisms that once lived on Mars. Other expeditions to hunt for meteorites have been conducted in the Sahara and Australian deserts.*

Impact!

As you've seen, there are many asteroids and comets whose **orbits** take them close to Earth. Very rarely, one of these chunks of space **debris** hits our planet. Although wind, rain and other forces have destroyed most traces of impacts on Earth, our planet has certainly been struck by comets, asteroids and **meteorites** throughout its history.

In 1908 a million-tonne comet fragment struck Earth's **atmosphere** at 97,000 kilometres (60,000 miles) per hour. The collision with the atmosphere made the fragment explode before it hit the ground, but the blast of hot air still flattened 2000 square kilometres (770 square miles) of forest in Siberia. This impact, known as the Tunguska Event, was visible more than 800 kilometres (500 miles) away. Luckily, Siberia is very thinly populated, so the impact caused less harm than it could have done. Even if it had fallen in the Pacific Ocean it would have caused a **tsunami** and killed people thousands of kilometres away.

A more deadly impact may have happened in 1490, when more than 10,000 people are reported to have died in the Chinese city of Qingyang as 'stones fell like rain' from the sky – perhaps due to an exploding **meteor**.

This artist's impression shows an asteroid over 50 kilometres (31 miles) wide hitting Earth. Such a huge impact could kill all complex forms of life.

Arizona's Barringer crater is 1.2 kilometres (0.75 miles) wide. It formed 50,000 years ago when a 10,000-tonne iron meteorite smashed into the ground.

In recent times astronomers have catalogued thousands of objects in Earth-crossing orbits, and more are still being discovered. The chance of a really large object hitting Earth is very small, but such collisions do happen. As recently as 1994, astronomers around the world watched as Comet Shoemaker-Levy plunged into Jupiter and exploded, producing fireballs bigger than Earth.

People stop their cars to watch a meteorite fireball tear across the sky in this scene from the film **Deep Impact**. *Sights like this are very rare but not impossible.*

The most famous impact on Earth is the one thought to have killed the dinosaurs 65 million years ago. Many astronomers think a comet 10 kilometres (6 miles) wide struck the Gulf of Mexico around this time, creating a crater 300 kilometres (186 miles) across. The debris thrown into the sky would have stayed in the atmosphere for years and deprived the planet of life-giving sunlight.

Mass extinctions like the one in which the dinosaurs perished have happened throughout history. Some scientists have suggested that these events occur regularly, perhaps when something in deep space disturbs the Oort cloud or the Kuiper belt and sends comets hurtling into the inner Solar System. If this theory is correct, we are currently in the middle of the gap between two mass extinctions, so we should be safe for a few million years!

Project Spaceguard

Astronomers are hard at work looking for NEAs that might hit Earth. In 1996 the International Spaceguard Foundation was founded to search for deadly space debris, and several large telescopes around the world are now using automatic cameras to scan the skies continually. But even if we can tell when an asteroid is coming, we have no way of stopping it!

Could humans live there?

Living on asteroids or comets would be a major challenge. The weak **gravity** of these objects makes it difficult to move around or work on them, and it is not strong enough to exercise our bodies – for our health, it would be no better than living in **zero gravity**. Any **mission** to an asteroid would have to take all its own supplies, and the ship would probably have to spin around to produce **artificial gravity**. A trip to a comet might be slightly easier than one to an asteroid, because of the large amounts of ice available there to produce water, oxygen and rocket fuel.

But why would we want to send people to visit any of the small worlds of the Solar System? One reason is money – asteroid mining could finally change space exploration from an expensive luxury into a business. Although the actual mining could probably be done by automatic machines, **astronauts** might be needed to set up and repair equipment. Cheap raw materials supplied to factories in Earth **orbit** could transform space travel and life back on Earth.

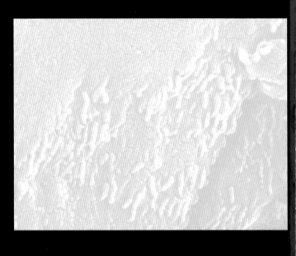

ABOVE: *Some scientists think the tube-like blobs in Martian meteorite ALH84001 are fossils of alien life-forms. If so, could comets and meteorites carry life through space to new planets?*

Comets might possess something of even greater value – the key to our own origins. Some scientists think that **organic compounds**, the building blocks of life, could have arrived on Earth from comets. A few even believe that comets might be cosmic deep freezes, transporting microscopic life between the stars.

RIGHT: *A space probe mines an NEA (Near Earth Asteroid) in this artist's impression.*

Glossary

artificial gravity force generated by a spaceship that enables astronauts to stand on the floor instead of floating in midair

asteroid belt ring of asteroids that orbit the Sun between the orbits of Mars and Jupiter

astronaut person trained to go into space

atmosphere layer of gas trapped by gravity around the surface of a planet

atom minute particle of matter

aurora colourful glow in the sky caused by charged particles hitting the atmosphere

chondrule small sphere of mineral inside an asteroid or meteor, formed when molten rock cooled billions of years ago

coma cloud of gas that develops around the nucleus of a comet as it gets close to the Sun

constellation pattern of stars, often named after a mythological person or creature

core centre of a planet, star or moon

dead comet comet that no longer forms a tail because all its gas has been expelled

debris fragments of rock, dust, ice or other materials floating in space

dense having a lot of weight squeezed into a small space

dry ice frozen carbon dioxide

Edgeworth-Kuiper belt ring of comets and icy worlds beyond Neptune, including the planet Pluto

ejecta material thrown out during the formation of an impact crater

element chemical that cannot be split into other chemicals

ellipse stretched circle, or oval

elliptical shaped like an ellipse

flyby space mission in which a craft is going too fast to fall into orbit around a planet or moon but collects information as it passes

galaxy collection of millions of stars held together by gravity

gravity force that pulls objects together. The heavier or closer an object is, the stronger its gravity, or pull.

impact crater circular crater made when a comet, asteroid or meteorite hits a planet or moon

Kirkwood gap empty space in the asteroid belt where Jupiter's gravity has swept the area clear

Kuiper belt object icy object in the Edgeworth-Kuiper belt. Pluto is a Kuiper belt object.

lander spacecraft that lands on a planet or moon

long-period comet comet that takes more than 200 years to orbit the Sun

magnetic field region around an object where a compass can detect the object's north pole

magnetometer instrument used to detect and measure magnetic fields

mass extinction event where many types of organisms on Earth died out at around the same time. Some scientists think mass extinctions are caused by comet impacts.

meteor small piece of dust or space rock that burns up in a planet's atmosphere, producing a streak of light called a shooting star

meteorite space rock that hits Earth's surface

meteoroid small piece of space rock that may become a meteor or a meteorite

mineral type of solid chemical found in rock

mission expedition to visit a specific target in space, such as a planet, moon or comet

mission control headquarters from which a mission is monitored and controlled

NEA (Near Earth Asteroid) asteroid with an orbit that brings it close to Earth

nucleus solid lump of ice in the centre of a comet

orbit path an object takes around another when it is trapped by the heavier object's gravity; or, to take such a path

organic compound substance made up of molecules containing carbon atoms

particle tiny fragment of an atom. Particle can also mean a speck of dust or dirt.

planetesimal small, planet-like ball of debris that formed in the early Solar System

radar technology that uses short pulses of radio waves to calculate an object's position or shape

radiation energy released in rays from a source. Heat and light are types of radiation.

regolith layer of dust and rock fragments on an asteroid, planet or moon, formed during impacts

shockwave powerful pulse of energy that spreads out from an explosion, collision or other source

short-period comet comet that orbits the Sun in less than 200 years

solar flare sudden burst of gas and radiation from the Sun

solar wind stream of electrified gas that flies out of the Sun and across space at very high speed

space probe robotic vehicle sent from Earth to study the Solar System

spectrometer instrument used to detect and measure different types of light in spectroscopy

spectroscopy analysis of the chemicals in an object based on the type of light the object reflects

trailing side side of a planet that faces away from the direction of travel

tsunami extremely powerful and destructive ocean wave, sometimes incorrectly called a tidal wave

vacuum space where no matter exists

volatile able to turn into a gas easily

X-ray type of invisible radiation that can penetrate matter too dense for light rays to pass through

zero gravity absence of gravity in space, causing objects to become weightless and float in midair

Books and websites

Englebert, Phyllis. *The Handy Space Answer Book*. London: The Gale Group, 1997.
Furniss, Tim. *The Solar System – Spinning Through Space*. London: Hodder Wayland (Hodder & Stoughton Children's Division), 1999.
near.jhuapl.edu/ – NEAR home page
nssdc.gsfc.nasa.gov/photo_gallery/ – NASA NSSDC Photo Gallery
sci.esa.int/home/rosetta/index.cfm – Rosetta home page
seds.lpl.arizona.edu/nineplanets/nineplanets/nineplanets.html – Nine Planets home page
www.jpl.nasa.gov/sl9/ – Comet Shoemaker-Levy home page

Index

Picture Credits
Key: t – top, b – below, c – centre, l – left, r – right. **NASA**: 3b, 4–5b, 6, 9t, 12t, 12b, 16, 36t, 36b, GSFC/NOAA/USGS 10br, JPL/California Institute of Technology 29b; **SOHO***: 4l; **The Art Archive**: Scrovegni Chapel Padua/Dagli Orti 26t; **Corbis**: Jonathan Blair 19b, Roger Ressmeyer 17b, Adam Woolfitt 14; **Kobal Collection**: Dreamworks/Paramount 34t, 35t, UA/EON/Danjaq 15b; **Mary Evans Picture Library**: 10t, 15t, 27t; **Science Photo Library**: Michael Abbey 33t, Julian Baum 8, 28b, Chris Butler 1, 18b, 32, John Chumak 26b, European Space Agency 28t, 29t, Jack Finch 20l, Gordon Garrard 20r, David Hardy 18bl, Steve Jay 31b, John Hopkins Univ. Applied Physics Lab. 2, 17t, Claus Lunau/Foci/Bonnier Publications 22, 23, Jerry Lodriguss 19t, 21t, Dr Jean Lorre 25t, NASA 11t, 33r, David Parker 34–35, Pekka Parvianien 30, Royal Observatory of Edinburgh 24, 25b, Dr Seth Shostak 35b, Space Telescope Institute/NASA 27r, John Thomas 3, 7t, Joe Tucciarone 13t, Detlev Van Ravenswaay 33c, 33bl, Frank Zullo 31t.
Front Cover: NASA, JPL; Science Photo Library, John Thomas. Back Cover: NASA, JPL/California Institute of Technology.
*SOHO is a project of international cooperation between ESA & NASA.